Highly Sensitive Person

A complete Survival Guide to Relieve Anxiety, Stop Emotional Overload & Eliminate Negative Energy, for Empaths & Introverts

Sarah Howard

© Copyright 2019 - All rights reserved.

The content contained within this book may not be reproduced, duplicated or transmitted without direct written permission from the author or the publisher.

Under no circumstances will any blame or legal responsibility be held against the publisher, or author, for any damages, reparation, or monetary loss due to the information contained within this book. Either directly or indirectly.

Legal Notice:

This book is copyright protected. This book is only for personal use. You can't amend, distribute, sell, use, quote or paraphrase any part, or the content within this book, without the consent of the author or publisher.

Disclaimer Notice:

Please note the information contained within this document is for educational and entertainment purposes only. All effort has been executed to present accurate, up to date, and reliable, complete information. No warranties of any kind are declared or implied. Readers acknowledge that the author isn't engaging in the rendering of legal, financial, medical or professional advice. The content within this book has been derived from various sources. Please consult a licensed professional before attempting any techniques outlined in this book.

By reading this document, the reader agrees that under no circumstances are is the author responsible for any losses, direct or indirect, which are incurred as a result of the use of information contained within this document, including, but not limited to, — errors, omissions, or inaccuracies.

Table of Contents

Introduction	6
Chapter 1: The Way of The Empath	13
Chapter 2: Empath Signs	22
Chapter 3: The Empath Phenomenon	44
Chapter 4: Energy Healing Practices	51
Chapter 5: Learning to control your energy	66
Chapter 6: Designing Your Healing Dream	76
Chapter 7: The Healing of Your Past	82
Chapter 8: Healing your inner child	90
Chapter 9: Healing Your Present Self	97
Chapter 10: Practicing Social Healing	103
Conclusion	110

Introduction

"You're too sensitive!" they say. *"You just need to grow a thicker skin."* You hear from well-meaning friends and family. If this sound familiar and you find yourself struggling with self-acceptance and feelings of shame, you could be what's known as a Highly Sensitive Person (HSP) – otherwise known as an Empath.

As someone who bears this gift herself, the author, Sarah Howard has struggled with the ups and downs of feeling like she was at the mercy of other's emotions. On a cold December morning in 2014, while everyone (including Sarah herself) where in good spirits about the up-coming holidays, Sarah was rushing from shop to shop to buy the last minute gifts for her loved ones.

All was well until, whilst waiting in line, she heard someone behind her mutter "people that cut the line make me sick.". Sarah didn't take much notice as she knew she hasn't cut the line and so this lady must be talking about someone else.

"I said," she heard from behind her, "that people who cut in line, make me sick!". This time Sarah felt the outburst might directed at her, so she turned to politely correct this lady who was mistaken.

However, as soon as she turned, the lady started shouting in a confrontational manor, "yeah you! I can't stand the way people think they can do what they like and cut lines like they're the queen of the world!"

"That's not the case!" Sarah wanted to say. "I've been here the whole time! I've never cut a line!", but she couldn't get her words out. She was so shocked and scared by this woman's anger she was left unable to speak.

As the woman continued to berate her, Sarah found herself overcome with anger and fear and sadness. She didn't know what to do and found herself starting to cry. She dropped the gifts she was holding and ran out of the store, distraught.

Throughout the following days she found herself continuing to feel upset, and no matter what she did, or how her friends and family tried to help, she couldn't shake that sadness this any woman at the store has passed on to her.

This ended up ruining her Christmas day, as she was still tense, angry and sad from the experience. This only served to compound her misery and, after waking up on the 26th of December 2014, she decided – *enough was enough!* She was going to figure out *WHY* other people's negative emotions seemed to affect her so powerfully and *HOW* to regain control of her own emotions, energy and life – *once and for all*.

This decision lead her down the path of understanding what affected her and others like her in her. After years of self-experimenting, connecting directly with others and just plain hard work, Sarah has found what she feels to be the most effective and powerful tools to help other Highly Sensitive People forgive their perceived shortcomings and achieve their full self-actualization.

Now, maybe for you someone shouting at you for cutting the line might not elicit the same response. Sarah is definitely on the more-sensitive end of the spectrum of Empaths. But whatever it is you're struggling with in your day to day life, by better understanding your own and other's emotions and energies, you will be better equipped to tackle the world and it's inevitable problems.

This book is the culmination of this years of hard work and research and aims to help teach you the tools and techniques needed to develop resiliency in yourself.

Here's what to expect as you work your way through this book:

In Chapter 1: The Way of The Empath, we'll discuss the history of the term "Empath" and what it means to be an Empath in today's world. We'll walk you through what a typical day looks like for an Empath in the hopes that you can connect and relate to these experiences.

We'll talk about the daily struggles of Empaths, and also the positives of this gift, and how you can start to reframe the beliefs you might have held about being a Highly Sensitive Person.

In Chapter 2: Empath Signs, we'll cover the 29 signs of Empaths so you can see how many you relate two. This points are a great starting point for people just discovering their gift and should give you many "ah-ha!" moments as you realise there are others like you!

We'll further explore the positive and negative experiences of Empaths, details the specifics of how each aspect affects people's inner and outer lives.

For Chapter 3: The Empath Phenomenon, we'll delve into the research and science of the experience of being a Highly Sensitive Person. Amongst other points, we'll discuss the role that EMFs (Electro Magnetic Fields), Mirror Neurons and Dopamine plays in the life of an Empath.

By understanding the physical realities underpinning this experience, you can apply your gift in even more powerful and impactful ways.

In Chapter 4: Energy Healing Practices, we'll discuss the various methods that you can use to begin to heal your energies with. We'll cover some of the better known practices, like Yoga and meditation, but also some of the lesser-known (and very effective) methods, such as Chakra clearing and Crystal healing.

In this chapter, you'll be given the practical tools to start your healing journey, with guidance at every step on how to fully utilize each practice for the most benefit.

In Chapter 5: Learning To Control Your Energy, we'll discuss the steps you'll need to take to fully identify your own and other's energies. Once you have a solid grasp on the full power that other people's energies can have on you (both positively and negatively), you'll be more effective in controlling your own and other's energies.

For Chapter 6: Designing Your Healing Dream, we'll go into detail about the importance of your Healing Dream. We'll detail what this will look like for you, and how to design your own for maximum effect. This is a step that some people may call being "a bit out-there", but it's such a profound opportunity to take your healing to the next level, it simply can't be ignored.

Chapter 7: The Healing of Your Past. is all about delving into and discovering the effects your past has played on your current life and mind-set. We'll identify the life-lessons you've accumulated and discuss how these may help (or hinder) you in your everyday life. We'll round off by discussing the importance of, and the techniques to, live your life in the present moment.

Chapter 8: Healing Your Inner Child, will cover...how to go about healing your inner child, of course! This is an extension of the previous chapter where we delve deeper in the specifics of your childhood and how what you experienced helped shape the person you are today.

In Chapter 9: Healing Your Present Self, you'll discover how to take a step back from yourself and look at what areas of your life need to be healed. We'll touch on the importance of your new-found self-awareness as well as taking the final steps in releasing the pain and trauma of your past to live your best life. This chapter culminates in the outline for incorporating regular self-healing into your everyday life.

Chapter 10L Practicing Social Healing will challenge you to take everything you've learnt so far, and put it into action within social situations. This chapter is one of the "heaviest"/"hardest" to read, but, everything you've learnt up to this point has prepared you for life-changing steps in this chapter.

We'll discuss the importance of taking full responsibility for yourself and your relationships, and how this shift from victimhood, to a fully-empowered person will help you to overcoming many of the obstacles you might be facing currently in your life.

We'll close by reminding your that life is all about FUN! You need to take the time and give yourself permission to have fun. These mindset shifts, along with the on-going practice of "Advocating for yourself" will leave you confident you can heal yourself and tackle any challenge life may throw at you!

I would encourage you to work your way through this book at your own pace. Try to fully absorb the message of each chapter before moving on. You'll notice, once you reach the latter chapters focusing on healing, that you might feel you have a lot of actionable steps to take, especially if you still live in the stage of your gift where you can't yet identify and control the energy of those around you.

Taking things slowly and giving yourself the time to take each step ensures that you're not overwhelmed.

So, if you're ready to take the first step in understanding your gift and healing yourself at the deepest level, it's time to start! Take your time and enjoy yourself!

Chapter 1: The Way of The Empath

The term Empath has recently become a popular topic within the spiritual community, as people begin to realize that being sensitive is a gift and not something to be derived or ridiculed.

As an Empath, or Highly Sensitive Person (you'll notice we'll use these two terms interchangeably throughout the book), you have a unique gift that allows you to truly feel the needs of others, of the world and the of universe as a whole. This means, you have the unique ability to be a powerful, positive healer of the world. Your gift gives you the opportunity to feel where you can offer more love and compassion and then give this love and compassion as a way to contribute to this loving planet's vibrations.

Unfortunately, in some cases, life as an Empath can lead to obsessive behaviors that deplete your energies and prevent you from experiencing the real wonders of your gift. If you know you're an Empath, or if you suspect you might be, then you likely have many questions about what this gift means and where it comes from.

We'll explore in this chapter what it means to be an Empath, why you live with this gift and how this gift can help you live out the real purpose of your life.

We'll start with the history of what it means to be an Empath and cover the more modern definition to help you build your understanding of your gift and how it fits into the universe's unique makeup.

The History of Empaths

In recent years, the term Empath or Highly Sensitive Person has emerged throughout many different cultures as a way of describing people who were appear to be in some way emotionally or mystically sensitive to others. Empaths were regarded as gifted healers, philosophers and spiritual teachers in ancient African and First Nations tribes.

These tribes, known to offer their Empaths special blessings and compassionate treatment in exchange for sharing their gifts with the tribes, continue to regard them as such.

Psychologists interested in helping people around the globe understand Empath's unique gifts and how they can master these sensitivities, have recently popularized the phenomena. Dr. Carl Rogers has played an pivotal role in advancing the understanding of Empaths and empathic gifts in recent history by suggesting that this may be a parapsychological phenomenon. In essence, he believes that this is a unique way for certain people to understand and support others in their lives at a deeper level than previously thought possible.

"Sometimes listening to someone else isn't enough," Dr. Rogers says, "because empathy from others is what they need - Empaths, who have the highest degree of empathy, are wonderful in offering this unique support to people."

Being an Empath in Today's World

Life as an Empath in today's world is entirely different from how it was in the past for recognized Empaths. Empaths were revered by their societies and were offered constant support, compassion and respect by those around them.

However, seemingly in Western cultures, the inverse was true. People who experienced greater sensitivity than others were considered weak and were often shamed by their peers for their sensitive behaviors. As a result, society became grueling and uncomfortable for Empaths, especially those who had no idea that they were Empaths to begin with.

The understanding of what the term "Empath" means has developed over time, and many Empaths have been given the opportunity to explore their gifts with a better understanding of their gifts and why they experience what what do.

This also offers a chance to experience a greater sense of compassion for themselves, since they're now able to understand that they're not *at all* weak. In fact, they're incredibly powerful and have the ability to change the world as we know it by offering their loving, compassionate and empathic gifts to the people around them.

As society continues to shift to being more compassionate towards its sensitive beings, Empaths have the opportunity to gain a better understanding of themselves and their community's admiration.

Instead of being ridiculed for their abilities and personality traits, many are finding safe sanctuaries in the world where they can participate in society and play an active role in their lives. The era of being a cursed Empath who was considered weak is quickly coming to an end, as Empaths are now truly beginning to be understood and respected for their amazing gifts.

A Day in an Empath's Life

As an Empath, you might have noticed that your daily life can be very different from the lives of those around you. If you have yet to find a group of people who understand what it feels like, it can feel isolating, uncomfortable or frustrating, when you first try to explain your experiences to others. Your previous lack of the deeper experience of being an Empath means you're not able to fully convey of how powerful you are. Chances are, when you wake up, an immense amount of energy is instantly felt. You can literally "feel" the energy of the day from what day it is, which may or may not play into how you feel throughout the morning.

Your experiences of the morning can also play a significant part on your energy for the day. If they're positive, like being welcomed by your happy dog and having breakfast with your generally positive family, your energies will likely feel whole and nourished. However, if you wake up to a messy home, a spouse that is constantly grumpy in the morning or a sad child who has a nightmare, you can find you start the day with with relatively intense, negative energies that match those of those around you.

This can be challenging if you're consciously trying to face your day with a positive energy, but instead you find yourself feeling overwhelmed and drained before the day even starts. If you work or spend your day with other people, the bulk of your working day can be overwhelming, as you take on these energies constantly and feel them as if they were your own. For example, if someone arrives at work late and everyone is cranky because it's slowed down the workflow, you might feel irritable and exhausted, because you take on both your own, and everyone else's crankiness.

If you're lucky enough to spend your days working in a positive environment, you may find yourself feeling exceptionally positive throughout the day, but you might still feel drained after work because of how many *different* types of energy you encountered throughout the day. Whether your day was positive or not, the amount of energy you experienced around you was probably overwhelming and made you feel like you had nothing left for yourself.

You can spend your evenings laying low and doing nothing as a way to relax and allow your energy to fill up again the next day. If the flow of other's energies resonates with you every day, you experience the life of an Empath who hasn't yet fully understood, accepted and mastered his Empathic gifts.

As we progress through this book, you'll find that your life doesn't have to feel like this at all and that you can experience a more positive and enjoyable life without feeling depleted at the end of each day. In fact, you'll discover how you can generate even more energy for yourself so you can make the most of your life, while still mastering your unique empathic gift!

The Empath Calling

Being especially sensitive to others energies means you were born with an amazing gift that can truly help you change the world. You can be the person that helps to overcome the collective suffering that wars, greed, and ignorance have exerted on humankind for hundreds of years.

You have the gift of being able to fully listen to and understand people. You can support them in their healing journeys using your ability to experience complete empathy to an incredibly deep level. When someone needs love, compassion, guidance or reassurance, they know they can come to you and experience it. Since this is what the world lacks greatly right now, you're the perfect person to offer it to the world. You've probably seen this trend in your life with the number of people who have looked for support or compassion from you. This pattern may have become so regular that you find yourself withdrawing from or avoiding relationships because it can sometimes feel that more energy is needed than you have left.

This can lead to feelings of guilt or loneliness in your life, but it can seem like a reasonable price to pay to avoid feeling overwhelmed by your energy and everyone else around you. Empaths are often called to caring roles, often choosing to work as healers, caretakers, advocates, and teachers. This is because they have the unique characteristics that can make a real difference in the world and people around. However, their Empathic gifts, left unmanaged, can lead them to feel overwhelmed and unable to pursue these vocations for fear of being constantly drained and energy-zapped.

If an Empath is able to learn how to master their gift and use their empathic talents to their advantage, they will find that they can make massive changes in the world around them by pursuing these roles and entering them fully.

It's known that some of our time's most influential leaders, healers and teachers are Empaths. Oprah Winfrey, Deepak Chopra, Princess Diana, the Dalai Lama, and Mahatma Gandhi are all famous Empaths who have taken on their roles, mastered them and fulfilled their life purposes. This proves that it can be done and can be done beautifully as long as you take the time to truly understand yourself, have compassion for yourself and fulfill your own needs as an Empath and as a human being.

A Realistic Understanding

Once you understand that your purpose in life is to heal the world, it can feel pretty intense or overwhelming. On the one hand, because of your nature and the way you naturally interact with those around you, combined with your innate calling, you might find that it makes sense. On the other hand, it can still seem daunting or even impossible to take on such an enormous task if you don't take the time to visualize it realistically and put it into perspective. I want to remind you that *you're not alone*! Hopefully this helps you feel a little less intimidated by all of this.

You're not the only Empath that exists, and you're not the only Empath that supports the goal of healing those around us. There are thousands, if not, hundreds of thousands of other Empaths out there who are all dedicated to supporting this journey of healing that we're going through collectively at this time. All you have to do is learn how to master yourself and contribute in the way you feel most aligned with. By learning how to master your own energies, you can immediately make positive use of yourself and your purpose to change the world around you. You can do this by being a local energy healer, teacher or philosopher, if you feel like focusing on a more intimate, local-level would fit best with your goals. Or you can do it by carrying out a large-scale mission, like having a public talk show to reach the masses. (think, Oprah).

There are no rules to this and there is nothing that says that one dream or purpose is more or less worthy than another, no matter how big or small it may seem. You must trust that you were born with the divine ability to fulfill your purpose and that your purpose is your calling in life, no matter what anyone says or thinks about it. Some of the Empaths most important vocations came from innovating a new way of contributing their own energy and purpose to the collective and serving them in the way they felt most aligned with.

There's no *right* way to contribute. If you're still not sure what your personal calling is, you're likely to struggle to spend that time with yourself and develop self-awareness because you're constantly being drained by society's energy. Don't worry, when the time is right, your calling will appear and appear to you and all you have to do then is stay on track. Pursue your healing journey and do what you feel is right. It's going to appear before you know it and you'll have the exact blueprint for what you're here to achieve in life.

Chapter 2: Empath Signs

If you read the last chapter and felt a deep resonance with what you read, you can feel pretty confident that you're an Empath. However, you might be wondering what your empathic gift entails and what aspects of yourself reflect your gift.

Empathy appears in many ways, so you've likely come across many instances where empathy has affected or changed your life and how you interact with the world around you.

To help you feel comfortable and confident, and to help you understand precisely how being an Empath affects your life, we'll explore the signs of being an Empath and the common symptoms you're likely to have experienced in your life. This will help you determine whether or not you are an Empath, and how empathy affects your life. Although we'll discuss a number of signs in this chapter, it's important to rember that resonating with just one of these is enough. It's not uncommon that Emapths will feel a connection to three or more of then, but don't feel discouraged if only one or two fit your experience of life.

Each Empath is somewhat unique in the way their gift manifests itself. Therefore, you might find that some of these signs resonate more intensely than others. You might also agree to some extent with each of them. As long as you can resonate deeply with at least one or two of these signs, you're likely to be an Empath.

You'll probably experience more or experience these signs to a deeper level as you dive into your gift and embrace the reality of Empath.

The Signs of Empaths

People Point Out Your Sensitivity

Other people tend to recognize increased sensitivity in Empaths, which they often point out at different points in their lives. Your increased sensitivity may have been praised in the past as a wonderful sign that you have a big heart, or it may have been used against you in those who claim your sensitivity is a weakness. People who point out your sensitivity are a common experience for many Empaths.

Being sensitive to the point where others recognize that sensitivity can feel like a blessing or a curse depending on how others react it to it. If you have been made to feel intimidated about your sensitivity in the past, you might feel that this is a weakness and that you must try to be stronger and have a harder "shell." In this case, you'll need to focus on healing your inner child from these incidents of intimidation so that you can accept your sensitivity as a gift.

If you've experienced this as a positive thing in your life, like people commenting on how much they value you as a sensitive person, you might sometimes find yourself being exploited for your sensitivity. Although this isn't always the case, many Empaths tend to lean on pleasing people and "give" their energy through their sensitivity to maintain a positive environment around others. If you're around people and you begin to experience the emotions they're experiencing themselves, you're probably an Empath.

Empaths often report that they feel other people's emotions deeply and often express them more clearly and effectively than the other person could. For example, if someone hears some bad news and feels shocked and sad, you might experience the energy from that news through them, and more intensely than them so you may find yourself crying from the news, even though it doesn't affect you. This display can be even more "showy" than the other person who can struggle to feel and process his emotions effectively.

It can also feel overwhelming for you to be around people who don't know how to process their emotions effectively. You might feel a constant, intense feeling inside of people who tend to bottle up their emotions, which comes from having too many unexpressed emotions. You might also feel overwhelmed from people who express themselves loudly or aggressively, because the energy output is so intense.

Negative Feelings Overwhelm

Empaths are often overwhelmed by negative feelings. This includes being overwhelmed by other people's negative feelings as well as your own. Negative feelings often come with a heavy, dense energy that can leave an Empath feeling as if the emotion itself is literally weighing them down. As a result, you can be exhausted, frustrated and find it difficult to express yourself. An intense desire to get the energy away from you can lead to negative feelings being avoided or denied as a way to avoid facing this heavy density of emotion.

Something surprising is that many Empaths aren't fully aware that positive feelings can also become overwhelming. Positive energy emits at a high frequency and can lead to anxiety-like feelings, especially when experienced for longer periods. After an intense positive experience, it's not unusual for an Empath to feel particularly drained because the energy frequency was so high and intense. If you're an Empath who hasn't yet learned to master your gift, you'll probably find yourself extremely overwhelmed in crowded areas as a result of this.

Anywhere with a large crowd of people can feel draining, due to the sheer amount of energy you constantly have to absorb and process. You might feel as if you're moving slowly as the energies around you move at the speed of light. The two completely different frequencies can lead to an intense sense of overwhelm and exhaustion soon follows. Due to this, the desire to leave or avoid all crowds is something that grows within many Empaths in an effort to avoid the uncomfortable feelings associated with them. If you feel intense anxiety about crowds but you would prefer to be an outgoing and extroverted person, the internal conflict can be extremely frustrating when you try to balance your anxiety with your extroverted desires.

The good thing is that you can actually change the way you approach crowds and successfully engage in extroverted experiences and even thrive by learning how to master your energy and manage yourself in places with more busy energies.

In a world where everyone seems to strive to reconnect with their intuition, you might struggle to relate to this desire. To you, being in contact with your intuition has always come to you naturally, and you might be surprised that it's not the same for others. You have always experienced input from your intuition as long as you can remember, and it's always been right. However, whether you chose to believe it or not, it can be an entirely different story. Because of how "hard" society has been for so long, many Empaths blatantly ignore their intuition and instead follow what they were "supposed to do." This often leads to the wrong path being drawn and the wrong things being done that can lead to a myriad of problems and consequences.

If you have found yourself struggling to trust your intuition despite it always seeming correct in the end, you're not alone. As you heal your relationship with yourself and your higher consciousness, your ability to trust in and act on your intuition will increase, and you'll find yourself not struggling nearly as much.

Your Pain Threshold Is Low

Many Empaths find that their actual pain threshold for both physical and emotional experiences is particularly low. Getting your vaccine shots, dealing with a paper cut, or having a headache may feel particularly intense for you. You might have even found it to be so bad that you're embarrassed to experience these things around others for fear of how they may react to your response to a painful stimulus.

You might find yourself avoiding places with a lot of pain, like doctor's offices or hospitals because it's challenging for you to be around so many people who are in pain. Not only do the others in pain create a difficult energy for you to embrace, but also the building's own energy can affect you. You prefer to avoid these places as often as possible so that the energy of pain doesn't need to be embraced.

Your Physical Awareness Is Strong

People probably don't believe you, but you can feel sick before any symptoms even begin. You might feel that something creates sickness in your body and you can recognize what changes happen in your body, even if these changes aren't significant. You might not even be able to describe them as a particular symptom at times, because it's so subtle and yet so obvious to you. Headaches, gastrointestinal disorders, and muscle pain are likely to be the same. Some people may think that you're a hypochondriac because you constantly reflect on changes in your body and in some cases, you might be worried that something bad is happening.

When you try to explain things to doctors, they may struggle to get a clear diagnosis because what you experience is something that most people don't talk about, so they can't link the symptoms to any recognized disease. Most people probably experience these symptoms, but they don't recognize them because they lack the physical awareness you have. However, your concerns are worthwhile and, in the end, there's often a discovery of something that can cause your symptoms. The main reason they weren't previously considered is that your doctor probably didn't recognize that you noticed them earlier than others would have, so they assumed that the likely causes were unlikely.

You Find Media Or Images That Are Negative Hard To Watch

You probably feel extremely uncomfortable seeing images of cruelty or hearing stories of pain experienced by others. You might feel nauseous and nearly sick by the stories you hear or the pictures you see. You might also feel an intense outbreak of pain almost as if you were also suffering. You have probably created an environment in which you don't pay attention to the news, read tabloids or scroll through certain social media pages because you fear the pain you'll experience if you find a negative article.

Instead of risking it, you would prefer to avoid it and keep your energy safe and free from any sickness or pain from such stories or images.

You Can Spot A Liar

You can intuitively tell when someone doesn't tell you the truth. Although you probably can't explain it, you can feel inside whenever someone tells you a lie or someone around you deliberately holds the truth back. It's an energy that makes you feel skeptical and uncomfortable and supports you in your belief that what you said was dishonest. The energy of people who lie can feel extremely uncomfortable for you, so you can completely avoid liars. If someone you know or spend time with is a perpetual liar, you're likely to minimize your time with them, or find a polite way to end your relationship with them. The feeling itself is uncomfortable and can be very draining, and you don't want to spend time with liars. You avoid such relationships like the plague.

Stimulants or medicines seem stronger

If you take a stimulant or medicine, or anything else that might in some way "intoxicate" you, you're likely to be affected much more than the average person. Caffeine, for example, can have a particular impact on you by making you feel excessively energized whenever you ingest it. Alcohol can be something you have to enjoy in moderation to avoid overdoing it, and it can even make your empathetic gifts more overwhelming than normal in some cases. Many Empaths say they even have difficulty taking ibuprofen for headaches because they have such a strong impact on them. Due to your increased physical awareness, you might also find it difficult to accept the differences associated with taking medicines like painkillers. Whenever you feel them in your system, a sense of discomfort or anxiety can be created that lasts until the medication leaves your system completely. This can instead lead you to avoid painkillers and lean to natural remedies, which ultimately make you feel better.

Experiencing the symptoms of others

The ability to experience symptoms of other people is a common and sometimes strange symptom that people experience when they're Empathic. If you've ever been around someone who reported having a certain symptom, like having a headache, and then you started to feel a headache, you're an Empath. This particular dynamic can be challenging because others may feel that you try to compete with them and their symptoms as a way to get others' attention. The reality is, it doesn't happen. Instead, you feel so strongly sympathetic to this person that you take on their symptoms. The sympathetic pregnancies experienced by husbands or other people who are particularly close to pregnant women are a common and sometimes humorous case in which this happens. For example, if a husband is with his pregnant wife in the other room and he begins to experience what he feels is contractions, he experiences sympathetic resonance.

Empaths often get this, and sometimes they don't even necessarily know about people. Since Empaths tend to be sympathetic to everyone, they can take these strange symptoms from anyone, sometimes even without the person actually saying anything about the symptom. One unfortunate side effect of being an Empath is that you probably tend to attract narcissistic people into your life. Narcissists are people who have no capacity whatsoever to experience or empathize. Although they can effectively imitate signs of empathy, they can't feel it in themselves, which often leads to harmful and harmful behaviors.

Narcissists tend to be very abusive and manipulative, and their "victims" are known to be causing immense psychological and emotional suffering. As an Empath, you have one thing narcissists lack: empathy. Also, you have an excess compared to others. You're therefore an ideal candidate for them because they know that you're more likely to be empathetic to them and their internal suffering. At some level, you can feel the pain they have experienced, which has led them to be unable to empathize with themselves or anyone around them, and this leads you to feel sorry for them. Even if you can't fix them, you might find yourself trying to fix them. In the end, the narcissist manipulates and hurts you and the cycle never ends. You must learn to put an end to relations with narcissists and remove the belief that you're responsible for their ability to heal themselves if they're not willing or able to heal.

You might benefit from reading more about narcissism and understanding how these relationships are the way they are, and why they never change. This can help you end your relationship with narcissists and prevent you from entering into future relationships so that you can stop being exploited by people who cannot truly understand that they're exploiting you. You tend to be extremely compassionate towards others when they're suffering because you "get" them in a way that no one else can .

As a result, you'll probably find many people coming to support you. You might even find that people you have never met before seem to know you're supportive and Empathetic, so they open themselves up to you without knowing who you are. Of course, you still support them, as they suspected because that's who you are. Supporting others seems to be your natural gift, and sometimes you can even do it to the detriment of yourself.

Your empathy can make it difficult for you to recognize when you need to stop supporting others and instead offer yourself support so that from time to time you can give too much of yourself and energy to others.

You Experience Fatigue

Often the constant absorption and expression of energy in you and around you can lead you to a constant sense of exhaustion.

Sometimes the exhaustion may feel purely mental, and you might feel that your physical body can continue for a while.

This type of fatigue can lead to brain fog, concentration difficulty and an inability to engage in your environment. As a result, you can retreat to rest and do nothing, even if you could keep going physically if you wanted to. This doesn't mean you also don't have physical fatigue. In fact, even after a day of doing almost nothing, you might feel completely mentally and physically exhausted. If you're surrounded by too many people, just sitting at a desk can seem physically and mentally exhausting.

Even a basic outing like grocery shopping or clothing shopping can overwhelm you and make you feel like you can't work without a good rest. While other people do things at all hours of the day, you can plan your outings around rest periods so that after all the exhaustion you experience, you can slow down and catch up.

Your Inner Life Is Very Vibrant

Empaths tend to have a very vibrant inner world. You can find yourself rich in visions, dreams, ideas, and hopes that you regularly maintain and cultivate. If you're left to your own devices, these inner experiences are likely to envelop you in spending time dreaming, creating or enjoying more mystical experiences like astral travel or lucid dreaming. Unlike others, you find yourself enriching and enjoyable because of the many things you need to think about, dream and create. In fact, you might find that you're overwhelmed and frustrated if you don't have enough time alone to engage in your inner world.

You regularly schedule a time to be alone and enjoy things by yourself, which helps you feel enriched and lively so that you can enjoy life more vibrantly and with more fulfillment.

You experience sensitivity to sounds and sensations

If you're not careful, sounds and sensations tend to create extremely overwhelming energies in you. As an Empath, you might find that you feel overwhelmed and exhausted by certain sounds or the volume of different sounds. Some sounds and sensations can also stimulate other sensations within you that create a sense of pain or discomfort.

Many people understand that listening to nails on a chalkboard or the jiggling of keys can make their spine shiver. You probably have many triggers for these types of uncomfortable sensations that aren't strictly related to sounds. You might also find that other sounds or sensations create an incredibly good sensation in you. For example, some relaxing soundtracks can almost instantly make you feel a real sense of calm that can easily override any emotion you experienced before.

You can find different sounds and textures in your environment, as well as lights and visual aids to create these positive and pleasant sensations.

You can feel extremely overwhelmed and exhausted by trying to achieve too many different things at once.

Trying to do something as simple as eating and watching a movie, for example, can feel overwhelming. This can be worsened when you try to combine too many different things, like completing a task while holding a conversation and simultaneously trying to write down notes about something. Or, if you go shopping for groceries and try to keep track of your list while navigating a busy aisle and listening to your husband, you might be especially overwhelmed. Often, when you try to do too many things at once, you feel frustrated and irritated by the feelings of overwhelming. You might find that when you multi-task, you may tell someone else something unkind or harsh because you find it difficult to focus and you feel frustrated.

This can lead to feelings of guilt and even more frustration, leading to a strong and challenging spiral of negativity from your multi-task attempt. Since you know that multi-tasking can cause so much frustration, you probably try to avoid it at all costs.

You have to manage your environment.

It's not unusual for an Empath to feel like managing their own environment. Trying to gain a sense of control over your environment by managing everything and everyone who enters it's probably your way to ensure that the energies aren't overwhelming.

If you're in an environment you're struggling to manage, you might feel like you have to leave the environment because you just can't effectively interfere with it. In your home, you're probably pretty particular about not only how things look, but also how they feel. You're probably decorating and organizing in a way that feels good to you, even if it doesn't necessarily make sense for anyone else. Your environment may look confused or disoriented to others, but it looks perfect for you.

You don't enjoy being around selfish people

When you're around someone who acts in a self-centered way, you probably immediately try to leave that interaction. Egoists tend to create feelings of frustration and anxiety in Empaths because they can become energetic vampires that absorb your energy.

This may feel draining, overwhelming and exhausting. If you have a relationship with someone who is selfish and you can't end it, like a relationship with a selfish boss or sibling, you might try to create as much distance as possible in that relationship. You feel as if you can avoid being drained by this person by avoiding them, minimizing the time you spend communicating and trying to buffer your encounters with another person.

You can feel things you don't feel

Others may say it's weird, but you can feel the energy of the things around you. Things that don't even have feelings, like inanimate objects or certain days of the week, can have a very real and strong energy in your mind. For example, if you see a toy on the wrong shelf and a group of the same toys on a different shelf, you might feel obliged to return the strangely placed object to the other group. It can feel sad or lonely for you, so you have to put it back with the rest of your "friends.".

Things like days of the week, seasons, and even specific words all have the energy for you. For example, if you were to wake up on a Sunday, it would have a completely different energy than a Tuesday based on the day itself, regardless of the content of your calendar or the mood of someone around you. You can also feel a sense of joy at certain positive words and a sense of nagging suffering at certain negative words. These energies may not make sense to anyone but you, but you're sure you can feel them, and they have a great impact on you.

Listening is one of your strengths

You're a great listener in any conversation. You can intuitively "hear" everything the person doesn't say above what they say, which leads you to know what they mean or feel, even if they have struggled to communicate effectively. This ability to hear unspoken information means that you can understand people in a way other people don't.

People often feel very well received around you and as if they can express themselves more authentically because they know that you "get it." You can even be actively involved in a career or hobbies that revolve around listening because you're so good at it. It can be fascinating for you to listen to people and hear everything they do and don't say and give them a sense of true understanding. This is especially true if you have the healer's or teacher's Empathetic call. In your rich inner world and your constant energy alertness can often create incredibly wonderful and enriching life experiences. However, in certain circumstances, it could also make you feel extremely bored and withdrawn.

Trying to perform everyday tasks, like listening to board meetings or entering data into computers can be extremely boring for you because your mind wants to be actively involved and work. It's used to being "on the go" so it gets frustrated and tries to find new things to do whenever you're stationary or slowed down. You can regularly lean towards more enriching experiences that draw your natural talents for communication or creation as a way to curb your boredom.

These types of experiences enable you to play more enjoyably with energy and help you feel better in your life. You can feel your energy coming out to play when you engage in these experiences, and the experience probably fulfills your whole sense of being with feelings of joy and satisfaction.

Many Empaths experience an introverted lifestyle because they struggle to engage in active or overwhelming environments. Empaths who are naturally shy or unable to manage their energy more healthily tend to isolate themselves from the excessively energetic external world. Empaths can minimize the amount of energy around them and feel more confident in controlling themselves and their responses to it by retreating into an introverted lifestyle. Even Empaths who want to be extroverted are likely to retreat as a way to save themselves from the world's external energies.

This can lead to feelings of inner conflict and frustration as the Empath struggles to decide whether to go out and get involved in the world and feel overwhelmed or stay at home and take care of their energies.

Intimate relationships may feel overwhelming

For some Empaths, it can be particularly overwhelming to engage in intimate relations. The intimate relationship can feel like an energy pit where Empath needs to invest more of itself than it can comfortably, even if the relationship follows a healthy dynamic. For an Empath who is used to living alone or alone, it can be overwhelming and frustrating to welcome someone new to their space. They can find themselves completely avoiding intimate relationships so that they can control their personal space more effectively.

If you feel that intimate relationships are especially challenging for you, Empaths who aren't yet clear on how to establish and maintain healthy energy boundaries between themselves and others are likely to experience a common setback. As you learn to heal your energies and assert your boundaries, building and nurturing intimate relationships will be much easier for you.

Nature often feels amazing to you

Empaths have amazing experiences in nature. While nature itself is beautiful for anyone who chooses to enjoy time in it, Empaths can enter nature as a way to nurture their sense of well-being and release the energy accumulations they may experience.

Nature is a base for Empaths to go to that helps them finally feel free to be as they should be. If you find that nature itself is like a friend who helps you to live your best life, it's likely that nature is where you finally have the opportunity to feel peaceful in your life. Spending plenty of time in nature can help you feel nurtured and healed so that you can fully enjoy your life. You can also bring nature indoors with house plants and animals that can help you feel connected to nature's beauty without spending all your time outdoors.

You've got a big heart

You're probably a loving and kind person. Empaths are known for their great hearts and their ability to show love without reserve or inhibition to many different people. Empaths rarely feel that love must be "earned" or given in any slow way.

They're glad to share their love and kindness with anyone with whom they can cross paths and do so with their own heart's generosity. Empaths don't distribute large amounts of love because they expect to be loved back, but because the energy of love fulfills an Empath and they love to share it with everyone. If you find yourself dropping love notes here and there and the heart emoji is one of your most used emojis, you're likely to be an Empath. Your desire to spread love everywhere comes from your inner divine purpose of love and compassion to heal the collective. The more you share your love with those around you, the better you'll feel.

Your Search for Truth

Empaths strongly dislike the energy of lies and dishonesty, so much so that they often find themselves searching for the truth in life. They like to surround themselves with honest people who also pursue the truth, as their energy tends to feel more "pure" and "clean". Empaths can easily detect the dishonesty they're taught in the media, politics and even in education. They rarely fall into society's traps and almost always seek ways to embody and embrace collective truth and personal truth in their own lives.

If you're skeptical about what the collective tends to regard as "true" and regularly seek ways to understand what the real truth is, you're likely to be an Empath who seeks honesty. By finding honesty, Empaths can support society by healing, teaching and advocating the truth and ending many of the various sufferings faced by society. We're constantly moving towards a new, healthier society thanks to Empaths.

You experience frequent swings in mood

You can experience frequent mood swings as an Empath who isn't actively aware of how they can manage their own energy field in any different situation. Mood swings arise as a result of the people around you sapping your energy. This is just like experiencing the symptoms of other people, except that you also have emotions. You might find this symptom increased in larger crowds or in particularly emotional environments.

This is because many more people are surrounded by emotions that affect your energy. In quiet and calm environments, though, it can still happen. Even simple weather changes, the hour on the clock, or the energy of your environment (or social media news feeds) can affect your energy, which then affects your mood.

Beating around the Bush

Empaths don't commonly beat around the bush. They realize that holding the truth back or trying to tell it in a nicer way can defeat the message's purpose and prevent the other person from fully understanding it. Even if it's hard and uncomfortable, it's almost always said by an Empath.

Chapter 3: The Empath Phenomenon

The phenomenon of empathy is a way for psychologists and psychiatrists to look into the world of Empathic gifts and discover why all Empaths feel, think and act in the same way. Researchers have discovered five main reasons why Empaths are this way by looking into the minds of Empaths. They found out how the mirror neuron system, electromagnetic fields, emotional infection, increased sensitivity to dopamine and synesthesia all come together to support Empaths with their gifts.

There's a science behind your gifts that explains why they work and how they affect you. We'll explore these five factors in this chapter and discover how they help you to be an Empath. This will help you to feel more confident about your gift by realizing that it's very normal and experienced by many people. By understanding the science of Empaths, we can also discover how healing can take place so that you can heal yourself and experience life as a strong Empath that thrives every day. You don't have to feel like you're suffering from your sensitivity – *you can embrace it*.

The Mirror Neuron System

There's a specific group of specialized brain cells in your brain designed only for compassion purposes. These brain cells work in a way that allows people to reflect other people's emotions or feelings, like fear or joy. We can experience compassion for each other with these brain cells so that we can support each other in many different ways throughout life. For example, if your child cried, your mirror neuron system would also make you feel sad. If your friend was happy with their recent promotion at work, you'd be happy *for* them, as well as *with* them. Through this ability to reflect the emotions of others, you can truly share your experience and offer your support in any way.

This helps us to deepen our emotional relationships and helps us to have a stronger sense of community with those around us. Empaths are thought to have a set of hyper-responsive mirror neuron cells that allow Empaths to resonate with those around them at an even deeper level. This allows Empaths to feel even deeper links with those around them, allowing them to feel as if they can feel another person's emotions or pain. Since the resonance is deeper and the mirroring is stronger, Empaths can even cry with someone who is in pain because they can so strongly reflect the emotions of the other person.

Narcissists, sociopaths, and psychopaths are in contrast to Empaths. These are people who are thought to have what is known as an "empathy deficient disorder", which means that their mirror neuron system is in fact underactive. These people are unable to experience unconditional love and tend to harm others as a way of feeling good in their own lives. They're known to cling to Empaths or people who probably experience higher levels of Empath because they long for Empath themselves, but can not produce Empathic emotions on their own.

Electromagnetic Fields

Science has shown that both the heart and the brain are actively able to produce electromagnetic fields pulsed into the individual's space. The HeartMath Institute claims that these electromagnetic fields are capable of transmitting information to other people about the energy of a person, like their emotions (energy in motion). In general, everyone can sense and collect information from these electromagnetic fields intuitively, even if they don't realize that they're actively doing so.

Empaths are believed, however, to be more sensitive to these energy fields and can often be overwhelmed by them because they don't know what is happening and may not be able to tell the difference between their own electromagnetic field and that of someone else's. With their own electromagnetic fields, we can intuitively pick up the moon, the sun, the earth, and many other things.

Empaths are also thought to be more in tune with these electromagnetic fields, as with other humans. Most Empaths believe without a fraction of a doubt that the electromagnetic output of the sun, moon, and earth can significantly influence their energy and mind. That said, not everyone realizes that it's from the electromagnetic field supported by science that exists around different people and things.

Emotional Contagion

It's believed that a phenomenon known as "emotional contagion" is part of an Empathic ability to feel so strongly that other people too. Research has shown that the average person can sense and understand other people's emotions when they're nearby. In a household where one person comes home grumpy after a bad day, and then everyone else seems to feel grumpy, emotional contagion can best be recognized.

People can usually "catch" the feelings of someone else and spread over a group of people like a wave, quickly bringing many people into the same emotional experience. Psychologists believe that emotional infection is how groups of people can maintain great relationships: They can understand each other intimately and express similar emotions and connection. As you might have expected, Empaths are believed to have a greater ability to "catch" the feelings of other people through this very phenomenon. As such, they feel the emotions of other people in a particularly intense way that can feel as if the emotion is authentically their own when it actually came from another person.

Increased Sensitivity to Dopamine

Dopamine is a neurotransmitter known to increase brain neuron activity. Responses including pleasure are associated with dopamine. Research has shown that Empaths identified as introverts are known to have a higher dopamine sensitivity than extroverts. What this means is that a shy Empath requires less dopamine to respond to stimuli in their environment with pleasure. This probably explains why introverted Empaths are happier to do something quiet and relaxed than something outgoing: Too much stimulation that produces too much dopamine can lead to feelings of overwhelm and anxiety from significantly increased pleasure.

Empaths that identify themselves as extroverted are still particularly sensitive to dopamine, but the way they process dopamine is entirely different from introverted Empaths. Instead of feeling overwhelmed by excessive dopamine, extroverted empaths actually crave dopamine and find themselves doing things in search of an "increased dopamine high." This means that they regularly engage in active environments, join crowds and enjoy the outgoing side of life as a way of feeling encouraged and positive in their lives.

Synesthesia

A state known as "mirror-touch synesthesia" appears to be most aligned with the phenomenon of empathy. Synesthesia is a neurological condition known to combine two completely different senses in the brain. For example, if you hear a particular piece of music and start to see certain colors in the eye of your mind, synesthesia occurs. Mirror-touch synesthesia is an amplified variation of this condition in which people can actually feel other people's emotions and sensations in their own body.

The way they feel these sensations seem to happen to them when they're not in reality. An Empath would probably not know the difference, however, as they may not know what is actually happening. It may feel so compelling to them that they genuinely believe that something is happening directly to them affects their emotions.

This phenomenon not only explains precisely what happens to Empaths during their empathic experiences, but also gives a clear reason why these things happen. As you now know, being an Empath is a very real experience and is mainly involved in electromagnetic fields and synesthesia with mirror-touch.

The question now is: How can you incorporate healing into your life so you can gain more control over these experiences and stop feeling like you're trapped in a vicious cycle you can't escape?

The answer is rather simple: You have to start healing. One way to begin healing is through energy healing that helps you keep your own electromagnetic fields clear and comfortable. You must also focus on living your own life and taking back any control you might have lost through previous traumatic or painful experiences. You can take control of your energies and start living your best life by healing from your past and allowing yourself to regain control.

Chapter 4: Energy Healing Practices

Energy healing is one of the most essential healing practices an Empath can learn about. Energy healing practices allow Empaths to immediately begin the healing process without engaging in past, present or future psychological healing. Although these types of psychological healing are still beneficial and often necessary, you can begin to experience significant relief from your symptoms by engaging in energetic healing practices.

There are two ways you can choose to go when it comes to energetic healing practices that give you great support and benefits. One includes having a trained practitioner perform your healing for you, and the other includes working with yourself.

You should ideally engage in both styles to gain maximum benefits from healing. During times when you want to practice extra self-care or experience a more hands-off approach, an energy healer should be expertly trained in any modality that feels fit for you. Knowing how to heal your own energy allows you to stay in control of your energy and maintain an optimal state of energy health for periods between your sessions.

We'll explore the many varieties of energy healing available in this chapter and how you can use them in your own life. Many of these energy healing practices can be done by yourself or with an experienced practitioner's support so that you can benefit fully from your energy healing experience. If you have never experienced energy healing before, these practices can still be used to start taking control of your energy right now!

Acupuncture

Acupuncture is a type of energy healing that must be carried out in a very specific way by experienced practitioners. Small needles are inserted into your skin at different meridians around the body with acupuncture. Meridians are areas where it's thought that energy builds up and is sometimes "stuck" in the body. It's believed that balance can be restored within the body by gently tapping the needles into these meridians. This healing method is based on ancient Chinese medicine practices designed to help people release chronic pain and emotional and spiritual pain.

This modality of energy works with the psychosomatic system to support complete energetic healing in anyone experiencing it. Acupuncture can be done by a professionally trained therapist who can use acupuncture to take into account your energy healing needs and promote energy flow in your body.

Chakra Clearing

Chakra is a Sanskrit word for "wheel" or "disk" that refers to seven energy centers in the human body. These energy centers are located at the base of your spine, slightly below your belly button, in your solar plexus, in your heart, in your throat, slightly above and between your eyebrows, and at your head's crown.

Each person has their own color, name, and meaning for what these represent in your body, life and spiritual self. Empaths that regularly don't actively clear their energy tend to find their chakras either overactive or underactive. It's believed that unbalance in chakras produces an unhealthy balance within the individual in either state that can lead to negative or unwanted energy experiences.

For example, an overactive third-eye chakra (the one slightly above your eyebrows) can lead to excessive vision or mental stimulation. An inactive third-eye chakra can make you struggle to experience any vision, perhaps even find yourself unable to use your imagination or to engage in creative thinking. Knowing how to clear your chakras begins by finding and feeling them.

A great way to do this is to lie on your back, relax in a meditative state and hover your hand over your body about six inches. Begin by hovering over your root chakra and see if you can feel any energy coming from it. When you "read" each of your seven chakras, move your hand up your body.

Getting a feel for what your chakras feel like is an excellent opportunity to explore and understand your chakras and how they feel to you. You can start practicing chakra clearing with each of your chakras once you have located your chakras. Each chakra typically requires its own unique balancing practice if you don't use Reiki, which addresses each chakra in one holistic process. Each chakra can be balanced on the basis of which your body scan is overactive or underactive. Listed below is each chakra, with its correct name, color, meaning and healing practice defined:

Root Chakra (Muladhara)

Located at the base of the spine, his chakra is red and represents your connection to the earth and the lower body (i.e., legs, knees and feet). By walking barefoot in nature, spending time in nature or eating healthy red foods like tomatoes, berries, and apples, you can heal your root chakra.

Sacred Chakra (Swadhisthana)

Positioned slightly below the belly button, this chakra is color orange and represents your creativity and reproductive organs. You can heal your sacral chakra by swimming, relaxing or eating orange foods like carrots, melons, mangoes or oranges.

Solar Plexus Chakra (Manipura)

Located above the solar plexus, this chakra is yellow in color and represents your personal power and your true essence. The chakra of the solar plexus affects the digestive system. Your solar plexus chakra can be healed by spending time in the bright sun, enjoying a friendly fire or eating yellow foods like bananas, pineapple, turmeric or corn.

Chakra of the heart (Anahata)

This Chakra can be found just above your heart and is green in color. Your emotions are represented here and It affects the heart system and all blood flow-related organs. By breathing in fresh air or spending time with open windows, you can heal your heart chakra. You can also cure it by eating chlorophyll-rich foods like avocado, broccoli, and all leafy greens.

Throat Chakra in your throat (Vishuddha).

This chakra is color blue and represents your ability to speak to others kindly and clearly. Your throat, mouth and oral health are affected. By singing, sitting under a bright blue sky or eating blue foods like blueberries, dragon fruits or currants, you can heal your throat chakra.

Third Eye Chakra (Ajna)

Found between your eyebrows and slightly above them, this chakra is indigo and represents your ability to experience the spiritual world with visions, imaginative thinking and "seeing." Your brain and eyes are affected. By sitting in the sun or eating indigo foods like grapes and blackberries, you can clear your third eye chakra.

Crown Chakra (Sahasrara)

Located on your head and slightly above your head, this chakra is purple and represents your ability to remain connected to the source. It also affects your brain, body, and aura of energy. By connecting with all elements including earth, water, air, and fire, you can heal your crown chakra. The crown chakra is strongly connected to the spirit so that it's not associated with specific food sources.

Crystal Healing

Crystals are a great way to help you experience a healing, nourished body of energy. During certain sessions, like meditation, you can use crystal healing, or you can use crystal healing by carrying a crystal with you during your daily activities. Crystals and gems can help your body, mind, and spirit feel their best when it comes to energy.

Crystals can be used to remove impurities from your energy body, balance energies in the body or inspire and promote specific energies in your body. When it comes to an official healing ritual, crystals are often used alongside meditation by placing them on the body in a so-called "crystal grid." This is done by placing crystals on your body at specific points depending on where the energy is most needed.

Individuals have many different crystal varieties available, so the best way to ensure that you use the right crystals is to consider your energy needs (i.e., more loving energy) and to select the appropriate crystal for this healing purpose (i.e., rose quartz). You can then lay your crystals on the areas of your body where you want to send or remove this particular energy.

For example, you could place a piece of amethyst over your third eye if you wanted to protect your third eye. If you want a complete crystal healing, the best way to ensure that the right crystals are placed in the right areas to promote your healing is to do one with a crystal healing practitioner. Your practitioner can also help you find ways to use crystal healing at home so you can practice it on yourself.

There are almost endless ways to achieve this when wearing crystals as an opportunity to receive healing from them. Crystals can be worn for your clothes as earrings, necklaces, bracelets, and even hair clips.

Some people also use pocket crystals, which are small flat stones that can be carried in your pocket, and you can rub them all day long between your fingers. It ultimately depends on what you're looking for in your healing to choose the right crystals for your healing practices. There are crystals for virtually every purpose, so the best way to determine which crystals you need is to go to a metaphysical store and ask the store worker to help you find the right crystals. If you're looking for crystals specifically associated with Empathic healing, you should consider including seven great stones in your collection.

Black Tourmaline

Black Tourmaline, an excellent stone to protect your energies and prevent unwanted energies from entering your auric body. If you keep a piece on or with you, any energy that tries to harm you will be pushed away by the energy of the black tourmaline. It's best to wear black tourmaline as a pendant or in your pocket.

Lepidolite

Lepidolite is a great healing stone in the area of Empathic anxiety. You can reduce the anxiety about the energies you feel and experience with lepidolite so that you can approach life more deliberately and with calmer energy. The best way to use lepidolite is to meditate or wear it as a pendant on your heart chakra or third eye chakra.

Black Obsidian

Black Obsidian is another excellent stone to protect you against unwanted energy. It's a great way to gain the benefits of black obsidian to carry a piece with you or to keep it in your surroundings. It can be quite sharp, so it's best not to wear or carry this stone in your pocket. If you want to use it during meditation practice, you can also meditate with it near your root chakra.

Malachite

Malachite is an incredible stone for your energy body to deal with emotions and release emotional and energetic blockages. Malachite is excellent for anyone who regularly encounters stressful situations and must be protected from these stressors. Malachite is best worn as a pendant or meditated as it rests on the chakra of your heart.

Hematite

Hematite is known to those who wear it for many healing benefits. Hematite is an excellent stone for Empaths to help you stay grounded and avoid harmful energies that can try to access your body's energy. You can use hematite to prevent people, like energy vampires, from sucking up your energy. When you meditate, hematite is best stored in your pocket or placed near your root chakra.

Amethyst

Amethyst is an amazing crystal known for its spiritually protective properties. Amethyst can protect you from feeling overwhelmed by energies in your immediate surroundings when used in healing. It can also help to create a sense of calm when you enter more busy environments or environments with stronger or more challenging energies. Amethyst is excellent for Empaths to decide which energies belong to them and to someone else. You can use amethyst in meditation over your third eye, or when you go out to wear almost any form of jewelry.

EFT

EFT or Emotional Freedom Techniques is an energetic healing practice that an EFT practitioner can practice on themselves. The whole practice is based on tapping on your body with specific energetic meridians and repeating positive affirmations.

The idea is that you lose energy while replacing it with more positive energy that actually helps you live a positive and productive life. EFT can be easily practiced by yourself at any time once you have learned how. However, you need to use specific meridians and tapping patterns to gain maximum EFT value. For this reason, learning how to do it for yourself is the best way to learn how to use EFT for your healing benefit.

Reiki

Originally a gentleman named Mikao Usui founded Reiki. When people engage in Reiki healing, their practitioner can channel universal life energy into them as a way to integrate mind, body, and spirit and encourage natural healing to take place. The Reiki practitioner is therefore not actually responsible for healing but instead encourages the universe to bring healing benefits to that particular person.

When Reiki is practiced, someone who has been tuned by a Reiki instructor to Reiki energy is practicing it. This tuning is considered a necessary initiation to align the practitioner with spirit energy so that they can start their journey to heal others energetically. A tuned practitioner can practice Reiki on himself or on any other consenting person.

This means that if you wanted to, you could heal Reiki as a way to start healing yourself through the Reiki energy. If you don't want to be tuned in the healing of Reiki, you can still receive healings from Reiki practitioners. Many of these practitioners conduct Reiki face-to-face or via remote sessions that can be completed virtually anywhere in the world.

The reason for this is that Reiki practitioners only have to be able to adapt to your energy to direct universal healing energy to your energy. Since true healing comes from the Spirit, you only need to be connected to a source that is an innate gift.

Quantum Healing

Quantum Healing is similar to Reiki because it uses the energy of life force to carry out the healing practice and support healing in the receiving person's mind, body, and spirit. Although other healings tend to be based on spiritual knowledge and trust, the science of quantum mechanics supports quantum healing.

This healing method considers how quantum energy affects the body and how the energy can be concentrated, amplified and directed to promote certain healing benefits. Those who have received quantum healing claim that physical to mental and spiritual healing benefits bring many incredible results. Quantum healing often includes a specific breathing practice that supports the body's access to life force energy and encourages greater healing experiences.

Qigong

Qigong means "vital life force effort." Like Reiki and quantum healing, it works alongside the energy of life force to promote energy healing in the physical body. However, Qigong uses both breathing techniques and meditation practices to stimulate the practice of healing and encourage energetic healing in the body.

Qigong is a self-healing method taught and then personally practiced by people trained in Qigong. You don't have to be trained to practice in Qigong, although it's a good idea to have a trained practitioner to show you how to facilitate self-healing to ensure you use the method properly.

Qigong practitioners sometimes practice what is known as "Qi emission," a Qigong style that helps the practitioner heal your body & energy. These practices are believed to be just as effective, although you need to be around a practitioner to gain access to these healing practices. If you want to use Qigong as an energetic healing method to help you thrive as an Empath in life, learning how to engage in the self-healing method is the best way to ensure that you get the most benefit from Qigong.

Yoga

Yoga is a practice of physical exercise with deep spiritual roots. Yoga is a practice used to engage the physical body in different positions to stimulate the flow of energy and to support individuals in healing at an energetic or physical level. If you regularly participate in yoga, you ensure that energy flows through you successfully, as you also gain the meditative benefits that promote the flow of energy and life force.

You're probably already familiar with yoga and how people can access this healing method. You can easily participate in yoga by joining in a local class or by following one of the many videos online. You allow yourself to keep your energy body clear and maintain a more peaceful control over the energy flowing into and out of your auric body by engaging in regular yoga practice.

There are many different types of yoga so you can take advantage of the time you spend studying each type of yoga and considering which one can be most beneficial to you based on your unique energy needs. If you want, you can certainly mix styles, but most forms are designed with a particular style of teaching in mind. In other words, the energetic practices and meditative experiences taught in each style of yoga vary according to where they originate.

You'll probably find overlapping information in each form, but the way it's taught and the methods used to achieve the desired results vary from one style to another.

- Hatha yoga
- Iyengar yoga
- Kundalini yoga
- Ashtanga yoga
- Vinyasa yoga
- Bikram yoga
- Yin yoga
- Prenatal yoga
- Prenatal yoga
- Jivamukti yoga

Each of these styles focuses on spiritual healing in a way that is understandable and accessible to beginning aspiring yogis. None of these practices necessarily require you to position yourself in any way that can be challenging for someone new to yoga. This makes it easy to start with an incredibly supportive to maintain your energy balance and feel confident as an Empath.

Chapter 5: Learning to control your energy

Learning how to manage your energy is the first part of learning how to heal your energy. Learning how to control your energy as an Empath gives you the ability to have a greater say in what your energy field enters and how it affects you. This is your opportunity to overcome the feelings of helplessness and the mercy of other energies so you can feel more control and empowerment in your life. In addition to helping you feel a greater sense of empowerment, learning to control your energies will help you recognize something in your energy body quickly.

The moment your energies begin to feel overwhelmed, you can prevent them from building up and causing problems by planning yourself an energy healing session. Ultimately, controlling your energies requires three steps:

1. Identifying your energies
2. Identifying the energies of other people
3. Setting energy limits so that no one else can interrupt your energy field

In this chapter, we'll explore how you can start doing this in your life so you can gain personal control and feel more confident when you enter the world around you. One of the main reasons why Empaths feel vulnerable and overwhelmed is because they struggle to recognize their own energies apart from others' energies.

As a result, they end up feeling that everything comes from within them and they derive a great sense of overwhelm from the difficulty of identifying why or how it happens. When an Empath realizes that many of these energies aren't their own, there can be a great sense of relief. This great sense of relief can then be followed by a sense of frustration that knowledge of how to prevent energy from building up and burdening their energy field is lacking.

If you've ever felt frustrated and overwhelmed by the energies of others, you still haven't learned to discern the difference between your own energies and others. This is the first step in learning how to control your energies so you can avoid being "hijacked" by the energetic experience and feeling of someone else caught at the mercy of those around you. When you learn how to identify your own energies, it becomes easier to identify the energy of others around you.

This can take some time and practice, but the more you practice, the easier it's for you to recognize your energies compared to others.

The best way to start is to:

Identify your own energies

If you have a stronger sense of who you're and how your personal energy feels, it's easier for you to identify which energies aren't yours. Of course, your own field of energy will change according to your moods and experiences, so that your field of energy may not always feel the same.

For this reason, you should invest some serious time in getting to know your own personal energy so you can build a strong sense of what your energy feels like in different circumstances. It's as simple to identify your own energy as slowing down and tuning into your inner self. It's a great way to identify your energies to spend some time in meditation to identify what energy most resonates with you. Most people report that somewhere around their solar plexus chakra or the core of their physical being they feel their personal energy. It's thought that this is where our personal power comes from, so it makes sense for many people to feel their personal energy.

However, you can feel yours differently, so be sure to tune in and consider what resonates with you. If it's your energy, a great way to tell is to consider the feeling you get when someone says your name. This usually causes a sensation in your body that leads you to hear who is talking to you. The same familiar feeling is the type you feel when you identify your personal energy successfully. It's also a good idea to do small meditative check-ins during the day when different emotions or energies are experienced. This gives you a sense of what your body feels like when you experience different things like anger, fear, joy, gratitude or an excess of energy. At first, you might find it a challenge to discover which energies you know or feel like because, in this sense, you might have spent so much time separating yourself from them.

As you continue to check in and recognize what your own energy feels like, this sense of familiarity continues to grow for you and strengthens your ability to identify your own energies. This way, you can build trust in yourself and your body of energy while telling yourself apart from others. This process alone is a huge step in the right direction for an Empath.

Identifying Other People's Energies

Once you have successfully identified your own energies, you must begin to identify how it feels when the energy of someone else penetrates your body.

When you learn how to identify the energies of other people, it's even easier for you to draw the barrier between yourself and others in a way that allows you to recognize their own energy and your own energy. You've probably recognized the energies of other people to some extent, even if you don't fully realize it. I bet you can think of a person, for example, who makes you feel "off" the minute they enter the room. Maybe their energy is quite toxic, so whenever they're around you, it's like you can feel the energy in your own space immediately. You might even feel an increased state of fear or overwhelm, probably reflecting the toxic behavior of the person's inner pain.

Similarly, you might think of someone who has a beautiful energy and always makes you feel so comforted and welcomed in their space. You might even want their presence because it helps you to feel so relaxed and comfortable in your own life. Although not everyone's energy will have such an obvious and profound impact, you can experience the energy of everyone, whether you want it or not. It's until you take control of your own energy.

Learning how to recognize the difference between your energy and someone else's will make it easy for you to establish this boundary and maintain empathy without taking on the experience of the other person physically, mentally, emotionally or spiritually as if it were your own. The first step is to know how to identify your own energy, as this helps you to recognize your own energy immediately. You must then proceed and begin to identify everything that isn't yours, as this will tell you clearly which energies you feel belong to someone else.

The best time to practice this is when you start to feel overwhelmed in a public setting. These are often the types of environments in which the barriers between your energy and the energies of other people can blur, as you have not yet established healthy energy limits.

When you start to feel this overwhelming feeling, you have to act by identifying where the overwhelm comes from. You can do this by checking the same self-awareness checks you used to identify your own energy. First, you need to identify your own energy and develop a sense of familiarity that will help you ground and keep you in your own space strong. You must then identify everything that isn't your own energy, as it will obviously be energy that belongs to someone else. Spend a couple of minutes visualizing the barrier between your energy and the energy of others so you can feel confident that the two differ. This will help you feel a stronger sense of self that gives you the courage and trust you need to control your own energy field. You can take action in two ways once you have identified the barrier between yourself and others.

First, you can act by requesting that any energy that isn't yours inherently be removed from your energy field so that you can resume your own natural energy state. This will ensure that all energies that have penetrated your borders are removed from your field to promote a sense of trust and calm in your own energy.

The second thing you need to do is set energetic boundaries. These energy limits will ensure that other people's energy doesn't penetrate your energy field regularly. This doesn't mean you won't feel and recognize their energy, but it doesn't mean it can create a feeling that you're attacked by other people's energy.

Creating energy boundaries is a healthy and empowering way to protect yourself from the energies of other people without closing yourself completely away from those around you. When using energy limits, you ensure that the energetic exchange between you and someone else doesn't exceed what you feel comfortable and reasonable. For example, if you're in the presence of someone with toxic energy, your energy boundary would insist that your toxic energy doesn't penetrate your energy field. As a result, you could still see their toxic energies, but they wouldn't feel as if they were attacking you personally or entering your sacred personal space. This can help you overcome the experience of taking on the energies and emotions of other people as if they were your own.

The same way you create physical or personal boundaries, you can generate energy boundaries. Start by identifying where the border is and what it should be. For example, if you feel overwhelmed by negative energy, you can set the limit that the negative energy of other people can no longer be *your* negative energy. Setting the boundary is as simple as declaring it and becoming aware of that boundary, the harder part is your need to maintain that boundary. To support the boundary and assert it as necessary, you must either verbally or energetically assert it to others, as well as maintain it with yourself. When it comes to bringing negative energy into your space to other people, you can approach the situation in the way you think it will be most effective.

If the person behaves in a toxic way, it can be most useful to address the situation and verbalize your border. If they're unaware of their toxicity or seem to behave reasonably kindly, but their energy is still toxic, it may be more appropriate to assert an energetic limit. What this means is that you assert to yourself and your energy field that no toxic energies will be accepted into your space, and then you uphold this assertion by not allowing their energy to impact you further. It's also essential to stick to the boundaries. Many people believe that the only boundaries to be established are those between themselves and others, but this isn't the case. If you and yourself set a boundary, break it to yourself or to others. You claim that this limit doesn't matter and that energy can freely leak through it, as you won't prevent it.

This means that if you claim you don't want toxic energy in your space, you can't become toxic to others or yourself. You must work to set the limits and remove all toxic behaviors, thoughts, and words from your life when you interact with yourself or anyone else. Your boundaries are thus kept healthy, and you can continue to grow.

Why You Need To Stop Shielding Yourself

Many Empathic resources advocate the benefits of shielding yourself, and they're right to some extent. However, keeping a constant shield over yourself is both ineffective and counterintuitive to what you as a healing Empath are trying to achieve. If you put a shield between yourself and those around you, you try to ensure that all energy remains entirely out and that your own energy remains entirely in it. This means that you don't experience positive and pleasant things in such a pleasant way because you try to keep everything out. It also means you have trouble interacting with your own environment and enjoying it. Also, holding this shield can be exhausting and can add to the many reasons why Empaths often want to live an entirely introverted life.

Another disadvantage of shields is that whenever you engage with your environment, you produce an energetic "leak" in the shield, which means that any energy can enter or exit the shield freely because there's now space where the shield isn't maintained. For any Empath, this can be a very overwhelming and frustrating experience, especially one who can only understand his or her own gifts.

If you've ever found yourself trying to hold a shield, but feeling exhausted or struggling to make it "work," it's because they don't work in many cases. Shields are great for moments when you don't want energy to come in or out in a particularly toxic environment. However, the shield just won't be enough for your average outing or social experience. The creation of energetic boundaries as I outlined above is the best way for an Empath to engage in a social environment without feeling the intensely adverse effects of the energies surrounding it.

Through these boundaries, the Empath can feel protected and separate from everyone else and feel as if they can genuinely enjoy and engage in the environment around them. Boundaries are the most powerful tool you can use as an Empath because they provide all the protection you want from your shield without any energy leaks or exhaustion.

Chapter 6: Designing Your Healing Dream

For you to immediately begin to experience relief from your empathy, it's essential to create a healing dream learning to control your energies and engage in energetic healing. If you want to undertake Empathic healing, however, you need to start focusing on how you can create a long-term healing goal that will allow you to thrive in your life. The best way to do this is to build a dream and learn how to integrate it into your real life. In this chapter, we'll explore how you can develop your healing dream so that healing and prosperity can truly be incorporated into your life.

This is an essential practice for anyone who wants to experience long-term healing, so ensure you engage in this practice for some time. Because you're an Empath, your already lively inner world is likely to have a lot of fun engaging and using this practice as a way to create a healing experience for yourself!

The importance of a healing dream

Empaths who have not yet fully embraced the path of healing and living as a confident and prosperous Empath can still feel as if they're condemned to a lifetime of overwhelming experience and struggle to protect themselves. This can be an exhausting and dreary outlook that can make everyone, especially someone who is sensitive and feels things so profoundly, looks forward to an enjoyable life challenging. Creating a healing dream for yourself gives you the chance to dream of a life you'd love to live, regardless of what your Empathic self feels right now.

If you dream of being outgoing and committed to the world around you, it's essential to incorporate this into your dream. If you dream of traveling alone and staying mostly alone, it's also necessary to include this. Your dream's real goal is to identify your true innermost desires and give yourself hope that they can become a real experience for you. Empaths often learn to live their whole lives around their gifts, sometimes even giving up parts of their authentic self to avoid feeling overwhelmed and exhausted.

You want your dream to help you learn how to live your life and to be an Empath in your life. The big difference here is that a person allows his gift to rule his life in the former experience, and in the latter experience that person takes control and rules his own life. Your dream is about creating a real visual of yourself living your best life so that you can make this vision your goal. This is your vision you'll hold on to so that you can begin to heal and overcome the problems that have held you back so far. Whenever you struggle to move forward or to recover, this vision will help you to find out what next steps need to be taken so that you can evolve in a way that includes healing your fears and regaining control.

How to design your healing dream

Creating your healing dream is as easy as sitting with your daydreams and dreaming about what you want to happen in your life. However, because you want this dream to remain somewhat consistent and eventually come true, it's vital that you take a few additional steps to help you make this dream come true.

These steps include: becoming very specific, writing down your dream so that you can revisit it as often as you want, and releasing the result so that you can still feel fulfilled by what you have manifested if your dream is realized in a way that looks different from what you expected.

Clarifying your vision

If you clarify your vision, you can see it and be excited about it. This also gives you something clear and specific to work towards, which is an essential part of making a dream a goal. When you dream without being particular, many variables leave room for you to aim for what you want or know if you're making progress. To clarify your dream, you have to spend some time thinking about who, when, where, why and how. Look to make your vision as real as possible when you clarify it. See if you can make your dream so clear that it almost feels like a memory for something that has already happened, rather than a dream.

This will help your mind to honestly see you live your life in this way, which will help you to manifest your dream life. When your mind can truly see and feel how successful it looks, it mentally prepares you for the changes you make and the challenges you face along the way. This is a powerful way to ensure success. In addition to dreaming up your vision, writing it down can also be helpful. Writing your vision in your journal or on a piece of paper and keeping it close is a great way to review the vision regularly.

It also makes it feel much more real as if you're writing a goal rather than just a dream. This helps you to alchemize your dream energy by transitioning it from the energy of longing to the energy of creation. The very act of writing down your vision also gives you the chance to validate yourself and your life's desires.

Many people create dreams, but then surround those dreams with negative beliefs or ideas that because of various reasons or excuses they create for themselves, they can not possibly bring those dreams into their reality. Writing your dream down allows you to approve yourself and validate your wishes so you can start building a sense of trust in your dream. This will help you change your hope into faith, so you'll go from hoping it's true to having faith. Release the result This may seem counterintuitive, but it's also important to release the result of your dream. The reason for this is that what we want in life often appears in ways we couldn't have expected. Your dreams will heal and evolve as you heal and grow.

This means that any dreams you might have held that were the product of the desires of someone else will be slowly released from your psyche and replaced by your real dreams and desires. It also means that as you evolve, you might be exposed to new information that calls you in a different direction from what you dreamed of. Allowing yourself to release the result ensures you remain subscribed to a dream that truly serves you and your wishes. Trying to heal yourself by forcing yourself to stay adhered to a dream you have made in the past will only hold you back, as this old dream won't help you at that moment to feel your best. Be prepared to release the result and allow the dream to reflect what you honestly want in your life.

You'll then find yourself living the best possible life. Apart from giving you faith and direction, effectively using your healing dream, your dream gives you the opportunity to start taking practical steps towards the life you want to live. You can use your dream to begin to make the next best move, to help you feel the way you want to feel and to encourage you to stay on track at all times.

Your dream is a powerful guide that can give you all you need to move forward and live your best life when used correctly. When it comes to practically using your dream, try to use it as a compass for your life and the choices you make in your life. Look at your dream and consult it whenever you struggle in your life to take action, change or make a choice. If you feel stuck, pray for your dream to guide you to your next step so that you can continue to achieve what you want in life.

If you feel doubtful in your dream or in yourself, spend some time visualizing your wishes and empowering your vision and filling you with faith and direction. To keep your dream practical, ensure you spend time actively allowing it to evolve. Whenever you notice that your dream doesn't resonate fully with you, spend some time considering what aspects of your dream don't resonate. This will help you keep your dream "up to date" so you don't get caught in an old dream.

Chapter 7: The Healing of Your Past

Empaths are often affected by their past experiences, which can lead to a negative ongoing approach to every day life. For example: an Empath who has experienced a traumatic narcissistic relationship may feel extremely co-dependent and struggle to live a "normal" life due to someone else's damage. This is true for anyone who has experienced trauma, but it can be especially challenging or harmful for Empaths who tend to internalize things and feel the trauma in a way that others can't.

You've probably experienced many bigger and smaller traumas in your own life that have made you feel like you need healing. As an Empath, you have probably been exposed to more traumatic experiences or events than other people. This is because the internalization of energy and emotions can be traumatic, leading to experiences that can be "normal" for Empaths. It's also because other people tend to recognize that Empaths are vulnerable and take advantage of empathy either consciously or subconsciously. You're more susceptible to adverse experiences like narcissists and energy vampires as an Empath.

Healing your past experiences will allow you to end the cycle of others taking control of you and give you the chance to retake control of yourself. When you combine the healing of your past with the process of taking control of your own energy, you create a powerful person. Your ability to feel confident and strong in yourself and to feel tender and compassionate towards others in a way that doesn't harm yourself is a mixture that allows you to heal the collective without draining your energy whilst doing so.

Identify your life lessons

By identifying your life lessons, you can significantly improve your healing experience. Life lessons are lessons that take root early in our childhood and appear through patterns we experience in our lives time and time again. Each person has his or her own unique life lessons to be learned, although your life lessons may overlap with the experiences of others.

Identifying your life lessons will help you learn and integrate these lessons into your life so that you can start living with a healthier and controlled approach to life. It will also help you understand why certain types of energy can affect you more than others, causing your Empathic gifts to feel overwhelmed when you're out. Whenever you experience someone's energy that triggers your life lesson, it leaves a lasting impact far greater than any of the other energies you experience. These energies left unmanaged, can be extremely overwhelming and frustrating.

The easiest way to identify what your life lessons could be is to look back over your lifetime of experiences and consider what patterns you see in your traumatic or challenging experiences. Identifying the patterns, you experience in your life will help you to discover what you might need to learn. It's important to understand that it takes more time and self-awareness to understand what this lesson is, as these lessons are often buried in our subconscious mind until we address them, evaluate them and integrate them. Once you have a general understanding of what these patterns are, take them for their face value and consider their lessons. For example, if you have been consistently surrounded by narcissists in your past, your experience can be to learn how to detect and protect yourself against narcissists.

This is a great opportunity to begin to integrate your life lessons and overcome these challenges so that you can once again take control of your life. However, you must continue to look at this trigger or lesson to see how specific you can get, realizing that life lessons aren't always obvious. Ask yourself questions like "how do I attract narcissists? "how can I fight to protect myself from this? "or" why am I in this situation vulnerable? "you can learn more about your unique circumstances. You might find that the underlying lesson is that you need to be more compassionate about yourself and your own needs, or that you need to stop trying to overlap and "save" others ' lives.

Identifying these life lessons and getting into the root of what they are, why they're there and how they can be learned will help you feel a stronger sense of control in your life. Instead of feeling deeply triggered by something and not knowing completely why or feeling haunted by a particular type of energy in your life, you can begin to take control and integrate this lesson so that these triggers or energies no longer bother you. As an Empath, this type of self-awareness and personal control changes your life by allowing you to stop feeling so overwhelmed by the energies around you. Healing your past and understanding your experiences are great ways to experience self-confidence and a better life.

How you can heal your past

The lessons of your life have been deeply embedded in your past and have probably had a massive impact on your life. For some Empaths, their life lessons can completely change their personality until they can integrate and learn from the lessons. An Empath who has been extroverted as a child, for example, but has endured many lessons that echo the same purpose, may be overwhelmed and anxious, leading them to live life as an introvert to avoid pain.

It's imperative to heal your past, as it will help you access your true self so that you can stop living as a victim of your past and embrace your gifts. Your past can be healed in many ways, although a healthy mix of approaches is usually required to ensure that you're thoroughly healed. It can also take a while to dive into previous trauma, discomfort, pain and suffering experiences as a way to relieve this pain and move forward in your life. Together with someone who can offer you compassionate support without interrupting your healing process, this is usually best.

Ideally, this should be a therapist who can help you with practices like talk therapy, although in many cases a trusted friend would also work well. I've listed five practices below that you can begin to release and heal from these past hurts. Make the decision to let it go Before you can heal anything, you have to make the decision to let it go. Getting into the mindset of letting things go allows you to move from the position of holding on to your pain so you can move forward.

We often want to let something go from our past, but we can't or don't want to make that desire a decision so we can do it. What happens is that, even if we want to move forward, we sit with that pain and continue to see ourselves as victims of the experiences we've had. In the end, we're the only person who continues to suffer. To make the decision, you just have to agree that you're ready to let go of your experience.

This doesn't mean that the experience is in any way reduced, invalidated or considered "OK" but rather that you're willing to accept it for what it's and move forward knowing that it can not be changed. You find the opportunity to begin true healing on yourself and in your life in this acceptance and willingness. Express your pain Now that you have decided to let go of your pain, you must try to express your pain. If you try to let something go without expressing the pain you have felt, you'll find yourself struggling to let it go, because there are still many repressed emotions.

Allowing yourself to feel the pain and express it productively helps you to move the energy out of yourself to continue your healing path. This is your essential step as an Empath to ensure that you no longer hold on to so many different overwhelming energies in your body of energy. You give yourself the opportunity to start from a clean slate by releasing these energies. You won't feel so quickly and easily overwhelmed anymore, because you won't try to take more energies on top of all those you already hold on to. You have to take responsibility for your experience in choosing to let go of something.

This means that you no longer choose to remain in the victim's mentality where you blame the other person for taking responsibility for your life and experience. This doesn't mean you take the blame for the wrongdoings of someone else or your own consequences. Instead, it means you choose to take responsibility for the healing process and let go of what you have done. This very process of taking responsibility moves you out of the mentality of the victim and helps you to take control of your life.

Empaths have a strong tendency to live in a victim's mentality when they still have to take control of themselves and their energy, which often leads to the belief that Empathic gifts are a curse. This is because you don't know how to take responsibility for yourself and your experiences. In this way, you can experience liberation from your difficult experiences so that you can start to experience a better life.

Concentrate on the present

After you chose to let go, expressed all your emotions and took responsibility for yourself and your choices, you completed everything you had to do with the past. You have to start focusing on the present and how you can improve your current life. This is an excellent opportunity for you to start considering the consequences of your painful experiences and how it's shaped your life ever since. You can also look at your Empathic gifts and find how your experience can make you feel some emotions stronger than others when it comes to emotionally and energetically taking over the experiences of other people. In many cases, you'll find that your most common emotions are directly related to previous painful experiences in your own life.

When you choose to live in the present, think about how you can start living your life in a more authentic and fulfilling way. Seek the chance to find out how you can continue to overcome the effects of your past pains so that you can live in a way that feels good for you. Choose to live in the healing light all the time. Whenever you experience something that would have triggered you as a result of that previous experience, make the conscious effort to let go and move forward in your life at that moment. The final step in healing is to forgive yourself and forgive anyone who has hurt you in your past.

Pardon is your opportunity to take control of your present and prevent your past self and people from your past from further hurting you. You might find that in some cases, forgiveness requires a regular commitment so that you and others can truly remain in forgiveness. It's essential that you honor the process of forgiveness, no matter how you look, so you can continue to feel free from your past pains. Forgiveness is truly a liberating experience as an Empath.

When you forgive, you alchemize the painful energy of the awareness of the victim and take control of yourself and your life again. This is the step in which you actually clear the residual energy of the past so that you don't feel like you're continually trying to approach life from a cup that is already overflowing with stress and overwhelming. Instead, you can approach life clearly and freely from your past with the ability to see things.

Chapter 8: Healing your inner child

Although you have already begun to heal your past, another key action is needed if you're to experience true and complete healing in your life. As an Empath, addressing your inner child and healing this part of yourself is an important part of healing. While healing your past will help to heal your inner child, other actions should be taken to support your inner child in healing fully. Your inner child is the part of you that still sees the past as if it lives in the past, and not in the present through your more experienced and understanding eyes. That's why it needs to be healed as an adult, regardless of your past healing. Healing your inner child is an incredibly liberating experience for many Empaths that support them in feeling truly and completely free from their past troubles.

This is the chance to completely overcome that small inner voice that continues to cry "danger" every time you see a trigger that even remotely reflects an example you have had in the past. By healing your inner child, every time you go to a social event or find yourself in a public space, you can stop feeling so on edge. When your inner child is healed, she no longer feels so concerned and afraid of the world around her that he can approach life in a calmer state. As a result, it becomes much easier to address and deal with any energy you might face in your life. For anyone who wants complete healing in their lives, healing your inner child is important, but it's especially important for Empaths.

Since you have been highly sensitive throughout your life, you might have plenty of memories to remember where you felt the impact of your sensitivities. The way people spoke to you, the energy they had when they spoke to you and even the energy of the environments you visited would have left a lasting impression on your mind as you grew up. This means that you have to consider even more healing than the average person who hasn't experienced higher levels of sensitivity throughout his life. The first step in healing your inner child is actually accessing your inner child so that you can start sharing communications with this part of yourself.

You can think of your inner child as a small voice within you that still thinks, talks and acts like a child, even though you're an adult now. For example, if you're angry and that inner part of you begin to experience the feelings of a temper tantrum, even if your adult realizes that a temper tantrum isn't a valid or productive response to your anger. Your inner child reflects this inner part of you, which still wants to respond to situations in a more emotional and less rational sense.

To access your inner child, you need to take the time to recognize that it exists and needs to be addressed. Allowing yourself to become aware of this need and to recognize it as a valid and important part of yourself helps you to provide your inner child with the safe space in which it needs to emerge. You have to start talking to your inner child. Talking to your inner child allows you to give her the attention he needs while understanding why she feels and acts the way she is. This is the very information you'll use to heal so you can start feeling emotional freedom and stop feeling so overwhelmed by your sensitivity.

Some people who are more attracted to the use of physical objects or their environment as a way to engage in mental and spiritual practices may find that it's easier to access their inner child if they have something from childhood. For example, looking at a picture of your younger self or sitting with a teddy bear in your childhood can stimulate your inner child and encourage him or her to come out and spend some time sharing. If you don't have your childhood belongings, you can always collect an object that looks like something you had in your childhood. Once you recognize and access this energy, you can start talking to your inner child and ask him questions. Some great questions to begin with include: "How are you? "or" what do you want me to know now?". This encourages this part of your psyche to start talking to you and to share information about how it can respond to the world around you.

For Empaths, this part of yourself probably has a lot of fear and anxiety about your adult experiences. It's a powerful way to start the healing process so your inner child can stop feeling traumatized by the world around you.

How to gain the trust of your inner child

You must gain the trust of your inner child if you want to embrace the healing process of your inner child fully. Many Empaths find that their inner child feels betrayed, abandoned, neglected or simply forgotten. This is because most people don't realize that their inner child still exists and needs support to understand and overcome life's challenges. Whenever you endure a new challenge in life or embrace it, your inner child will still respond in the same way as your childhood.

You still have an inner part of you that struggles to see, understand and respond to the world around you, despite the evolution you have endured. This part of you wants those around you and yourself to love, respect, cherish and appreciate. She also wants you to show her affection and be compassionate and tender, often reflecting something you might never have experienced fully as a child.

In life, our inner child often feels abandoned and neglected if she's not given the tender compassion and love she needs in these sensitive moments, especially as an Empath. As an adult, your inner child will naturally still respond immediately to these feelings, even if you don't recognize it or become aware of it. That's why your inner child has grown to see you as untrustworthy. It's therefore important to gain your inner child's trust. As an Empath, your inner child is likely to feel wounded because she continues to worry that she's "too sensitive" or "too serious." This part of you still stings each time someone tells you that you need to grow a thicker skin or recognizes a joke when you hear one, even if it doesn't sound funny to you.

Although you're now more aware of these experiences or more compassionate about yourself and your sensitivity, your inner child still longs for this tenderness and compassion. You can gain your inner child's trust by showing that you recognize that it still exists and that you're willing to acknowledge it and remain aware of it. By teaching your inner child that you have not forgotten them, but rather that you have not realized that they're still there, you can ask for pardon from your inner child and then work to gain their trust. In doing so, you bring your inner child more comfort. Trust your inner childhood self that you, yourself, are there for them now and want to listen to them, see them and support them in their experiences.

You must be incredibly tender and gentle with yourself and be consistent and devoted so that your inner child can see that you're serious about supporting it. If your inner child has been repressed for a long time, it may take some time to gain confidence and be able to fully access and listen to it. Be patient and continue to listen to your inner child so you can show that you're trustworthy. The more you do this, the more your inner child opens up to you and shares its feelings and experiences. This will help you to understand your own emotions deeply and why you're so sensitive to specific experiences as opposed to others or more sensitive to all experiences in general. Once you have accessed your inner child's trust and gained it, you can start working to heal it. The best way to begin healing your inner child is to express the emotions your inner child feels.

Allow all these feelings during these conversations to rise to the surface and be expressed wholly and healthily. If you have fear, let yourself shake it out. If you want to cry because you feel sad or shame, let it come out too. Use this opportunity to feel and release any emotion that wishes to rise to the surface. When you express the emotions that your inner child hasn't had the chance to communicate fully, you allow yourself to release the energy that this memory or experience entangles. This allows you to completely release the inner "bottle" that has filled over the years and restore a peaceful and calm state within you. When you release these emotions, you might feel anxious about the intensity of the emotions that arise.

You might be worried that these emotions will be overwhelming or you won't be able to control them. Trust that this isn't the case and that even when your emotions come out, you'll still be able to experience full control. This fear belongs to your inner child, and it's worried that she'll lose control because she was told it was wrong to lose control. Now you're an adult who can stay in control while expressing your emotions so that you don't have to worry about this experience. Just let the fear be expressed and then your other emotions will be experienced. You can thus experience a complete release of your emotions and release the incredible amount of energy associated with them. Your inner child is likely to express only a few things at a time.

After all, you have been a child for many years so you might need to recognize and express many years of experience. As you continue to work with this practice, each time you feel a greater sense of release. You might find that your inner child is satisfied over time and you no longer need to engage in such healing practices. When this happens, you should see that your ability to process life as an Empath is also much more natural, as you now have more control over yourself, your energies and your emotions.

Chapter 9: Healing Your Present Self

The next step in your healing journey is to understand and heal your present self. Healing your present self is an opportunity for you to release anything that can cause energetic or emotional turmoil in your life right now so you can truly enjoy life. Most of the time, healing your current self requires you to consider what your current state of well-being is and start healing towards your own vision. Healing your past and inner child will help you feel released from the attachments that have held you in this state, but healing your present self will allow you to release the symptoms caused by your past entirely.

The healing of the present self enables Empaths to begin to experience a greater sense of self-confidence and self-esteem so that they can start to enjoy life from a more intentional and empowered point of view. We'll explore in this chapter how healing your current self can improve your life and how you can use your better self-esteem and self-confidence to experience a better life as an Empath. Even if you're someone who already considers your self-esteem and confidence to be reasonably high, working on this healing practice will ensure that you use this strong sense of self in the best possible way to support your inner Empath.

Identifying What Needs To Be Healed

Before you can start to heal your current self, you must first consider what might be wrong. Looking into your past makes it easy to see trauma or challenges, as you can now see how they affected your life. Looking at your present life and trying to consider what may *"go wrong"* can be much more challenging because these are the behaviors, thoughts, and experiences you actively engage in. To determine what needs to be healed, it's useful to spend some time writing down the things you want to be changed or improved about your current life. Consider everything from communicating with others and yourself to dealing with different situations in your life. All these experiences contain massive amounts of energy that can affect your energy and make the world around you feel vulnerable or overwhelming.

When you talk about what needs to be healed, don't be afraid to consider parts of yourself that may have been affected by past experiences, even if you have already deliberately worked to heal these past experiences. Our past experiences often lead to current problems that must also be addressed. Just because you healed the pain memory doesn't mean that your behavior, thoughts, and attitude at this time still doesn't last. Addressing the present self, which also needs healing, will help you to fully heal from past experiences so that you can move forward and start living a better life completely free from all attachments to the past. You'll probably find many things to some extent that need to be addressed or healed. Even that won't end. Healing is an ongoing process that needs to be addressed and worked on regularly to ensure that you stay at your highest energy level.

Regular self-reflection and journaling are the best way to ensure that you always identify aspects of yourself that can be healed. This will help you to remain self-aware and fully committed to your practice of healing.

The importance of self-awareness

If you're not a self-aware person, self-healing can be a difficult process. To be able to heal yourself requires you to look into yourself and notice the parts of yourself that need healing. As an Empath, self-awareness tends to come naturally and inevitably help you on your healing journey.

You might also find, however, that if you live in the archetype of a "cursed" Empath, you have long suppressed your feelings and self-esteem. Some Empaths even report body experiences or dissociation experiences as a way to detach themselves from the painful experiences of empathy. In these circumstances, it may be more difficult for you to achieve self-awareness. If you don't already live in a state of self-awareness, you'll want to start practicing so you can understand yourself and your needs more clearly.

The best way to start practicing self-awareness is to check in regularly and ask yourself how you do something. Asking yourself such questions requires you to check your feelings, thoughts, and needs and then take care of yourself. This creates a strong relationship between you and yourself that helps you feel worthy of your time and attention. Like the healing of the inner child, you might find that you must work to gain your own trust to embrace the art of self-awareness fully.

Continue to show compassion and tenderness, and you'll probably find that self-awareness naturally comes from this growing relationship you share with yourself. Now that you have brought your desire for healing into your current state of awareness, you can start the process of truly healing these experiences. Since your previous traumas have cultivated all your current problems, you must finally release all your current links to the past. The best way to imagine this process is to consider the experience as weed removal. Your past and inner child's healing allowed you to heal the roots of the problem.

You must now remove the rest of the plant that grew out of those roots to make the person you are today.

Releasing The Final Bonds of Your Past

While you have an idea why you behave in a way that can help you to have a greater sense of understanding, it's not necessary.

What is needed is that you address every part of yourself that needs healing and begin to understand why it no longer serves you and how it can be changed to serve you better.

For example, if you find that you tend to be overwhelmed by certain energies even if you have to deal with them regularly, you can set your intention to heal your response around these energies. You can also determine how you want to behave in addition to setting this intention. Using your dream of healing is a great way to help you heal your present self. Through your healing dream, you can "see" how you would prefer to behave and begin to behave in this way. This visualization will help you gradually swap your current manners with new ones that will help you to realize your healing dream.

The process of changing these old behaviors is the last tie of the past that you officially cut loose. After this change, you'll feel like you're completely liberated from the experience that once held you in an energetic and emotional turmoil. This release allows you to feel more confident about yourself and your ability to assert your boundaries, including your energetic boundaries so that you can regain control of your life and stop feeling as if you're victimized by your Empathic gifts.

Incorporating regular self-healing

It's important that you understand that healing is an ongoing experience. You'll never be completely "healed" because more can always be addressed, evaluated and improved. If you want to embrace healing, you must be willing to embrace the full journey, no matter how long it is. Some parts of the process can be difficult, painful or just frustrating. Other parts may feel like you've been waiting far too long for the healing and you're excited to overcome your problems and start living a better life. In the end, your version that has undergone more healing sincerely appreciates your efforts. If you want to embrace a healing journey, incorporating your healing into your regular routine is a requirement.

Regular self-reflection, journaling, and dreaming are the best way to do this. The more you recognize unhealed parts of yourself and dream what it would be like to heal them, the easier it will be for you to visualize and then manifest yourself living your best life. As an Empath, using healing energy in this way gives you great freedom from the overwhelming sensitivity that can lead you.

Chapter 10: Practicing Social Healing

Empaths are rarely fully appreciated and accepted by our modern society as the world at large tends not to understand and appreciate the struggles of a highly sensitive person. Unfortunately, as an Empath in every day life, it may not always be well received to express your sensitive side. This can make you feel like you're not welcome in society. This can further aggravate your inner feelings of abandonment and neglect and lead to internal emotional trauma from your "broken" relationship with others in general. Learning how to heal your social experiences can help you engage in social experiences at a higher level so that you can begin to enjoy the public or the experiences you need to go out in public.

In this chapter, we'll explore how you can heal the feeling that society is outcast so that you can start to enjoy a better life and feel genuinely fulfilled in every possible way. Whether you're a shy or an extroverted Empath, these practices will help to support your healing.

Taking full responsibility for yourself

The first step towards better social experiences is to take responsibility for yourself. Learning how to take responsibility for your energy and experience helps you stay clear of the mentality of being the victim. This prevents you from feeling as if you're being attacked continuously whenever you go in public because you can choose to avoid these feelings of energetic attacks. When you realize that you're not disliked by society and that you're entirely welcomed into the world as it's, it becomes much easier for you to stop taking everything personally. You can stop feeling like you have the energies of everyone else and you have to take responsibility for them.

One of the worst beliefs to hold as an Empath is that you're responsible for any energies or emotions in your space. That's not true. Only your own energies and emotions are your responsibility. If they're affected or influenced by the energies or emotions of someone else, it's your responsibility to *recognize* this and adjust your approach to the situation to avoid negative energy or an emotional experience that is unwanted.

When you take responsibility for yourself, it becomes much easier to stop taking responsibility for others who help you to enforce your energy boundaries so that you no longer accept emotions or energies that aren't yours.

Overcoming the "sponge" belief

An unfortunate belief that the some communities circulate is that Empaths are "sponges" that constantly "soak up" the emotions and energies of other people. This is certainly what it can feel when you don't take care of yourself and your energies actively, but once you start, this symptom disappears, meaning that you don't have to feel like a sponge forever. Believing that you'll always be a sponge that constantly absorbs other people's energies and emotions can be extremely easy to believe, given that you felt it in the past and that others strengthen your feeling.

However, it becomes much easier for you to stop absorbing the energies of everyone else when you choose to take responsibility for yourself and your energies and start practicing and enforcing your energetic boundaries. It's important that you choose to foster a new belief as soon as possible so that your feelings of absorption don't continue to be reinforced.

The more you repeat this belief, the more you reinforce the meaninglessness of your boundaries, because energy simply passes through. In other words, you make your borders meaningless because you ignore them alone and allow yourself to feel unwanted energies. You need to take responsibility and get rid of the belief that anyone that isn't you has any control over your energies whatsoever.

Take responsibility for your relationship with society

Chances are that your inner child is the part of you who still lives in the fear and shame of society. This means that you're likely to need some healing about society and other people with your inner child. You also need to consider yourself as an adult and how you feel about society at the moment. If your feelings about society are negative, for example: you think everyone is too harsh and nobody appreciates or understands you, you'll strengthen this negative belief and struggle in society, no matter what. If you choose to adjust your beliefs and see society as a beautiful opportunity to connect with others and perhaps meet people who are sensitive like you, society suddenly becomes much less frightening and much more enjoyable.

You allow yourself to heal from those inner feelings associated with being an outcast or someone who was too weak for society when you adjust your beliefs in this way. You give yourself your freedom in healing your relationship with society.

Whether we like it or not, we live in a society and live in disagreement with the world will never help you feel better. If anything, it can make you feel exceptionally vulnerable to the energy of those around you, as you're constantly focused on others' judgmental, rude and harmful energies. As a result, each time you go out in public, your Empathic self will feel extremely overwhelmed. However, if you see society as an opportunity or a simple fact of life, these energies will cease to be so intimidating or frightening to you, and you can enjoy society easily and to it's fullest.

Allowing yourself to have fun

Empaths often struggle to have fun in ways that aren't directly linked to being alone or doing something silent and withdrawn.

Although there's nothing wrong with being an introvert or preferring to read or watch a film, rather than being with a group of people, it's not effective if you're the type of person who only chooses books or films because of your fear of society. If the constant worry of going out and enjoying yourself prevents you from actually going out and doing it, you need to learn how to completely detach yourself from the world around you so you can let go and have fun.

At first glance, this may seem impossible, but it is possible, and it can help you live a more fulfilling and happy life. It ultimately requires a commitment to yourself to allow yourself to have fun. In this commitment, you must ensure that you don't worry about the energies or emotions of those around you in a way that makes you feel overwhelmed or responsible for your experience.

Although you can certainly recognize their energies or emotions, allow yourself to completely detach yourself from them so that you can no longer feel their energies as your own. Then, just try to focus on enjoying yourself and the world around you without feeling so overwhelmed and exhausted.

At first, this might seem like an impossible task. It probably sounds difficult to detach yourself, because you might be worried that detachment will prevent you from feeling any emotions whatsoever. I can assure you that that is not the case. Cultivating a healthy detachment will allow you to separate yourself from feeling *personally* responsible for someone else. Among other emotions, you can still experience and express empathy, but you won't feel such a nagging and overwhelming need to engage in energies and emotions that aren't yours.

It can be beneficial for you to start practicing this type of detachment in environments that aren't so overwhelming at first, so you can get the hang of it.. As you do, continue to increase the intensity of your environment at a rate that feels comfortable to you, so that you can fully embrace your detachment at each "level" until you feel confident and ready to move up. Moving at your own pace will help you feel more confident about your control of yourself and your ability to detach yourself from your intense energies.

Advocating for yourself

If you want to be more involved in society as an Empath, being an advocate for yourself is essential. When acting as your own personal advocate, you must pay attention to your needs and wishes whenever you're out and about in public. This is part of your responsibility, but it's also an essential component to your healing that requires your own independent attention.

If you're an advocate for yourself, you must be prepared not only to identify your needs and wishes, but also to ensure that they're met. For example, if you feel particularly overwhelmed by your environment and feel like you need to step out for a few minutes, or excuse yourself from the event so that you can retreat to a more relaxed environment. It's never too big or too an issue small to address, no matter what your need is. It's never too unreasonable to ask – put yourself *first*.

If you spend time with someone who doesn't respect your right to express your own emotions and actively fulfill your needs, you may want to consider spending time with people who may be more concerned about you and your wishes. Ultimately, you're responsible for ensuring that your own needs are met, regardless of who you're with or what attitude they may have. You must ensure that you are an advocate for yourself and your needs at all times so that you can stay confident and be more optimistic about your outings.

Conclusion

Congratulations on completing this first step in your journey of self-discovery. I genuinely hope you have discovered more about yourself by reading this book and experience a greater sense of self-awareness through the explanations in this book.

By understanding yourself to a greater extent, you give yourself the power to take control of your own life and to experience a higher quality of life in general. You won't feel like you're living at the mercy of those around you anymore, the more you practice taking control of your life.

You'll find yourself, as an Empath, picking up energies that other people may not even realize. Experiencing these energies when the person responsible for the energies doesn't even want to experience them is a burden that nobody has to take. You must learn to take responsibility for yourself and heal the parts of you that led you to believe otherwise to live your best life. By healing these parts of yourself, you allow yourself to empty the "reserve" of unhealed energies within you so that you can approach life with a greater sense of personal power and trust. You'll access to your best life through that. After reading this book, it's essential that you continue to master your empathic gift.

The more you heal and take your power back while strengthening your personal energy, the easier it will be for you to master your gift. You can then step into your real calling to be a healer, teacher, caretaker or whichever profession feels like it resonates with you the most.

If you can accept this call from a place of power, you'll begin to discover ways in which your empathic gift can genuinely help you rather than hinder you from complete success. Any Empath who tries to embrace their true calling without mastering the gift of being an Empath will quickly feel burnt out by following their passion.

This can lead to a myriad of new problems, including the need to experience further healing, especially around their desires, in their lives. To avoid burnout and exhaustion, first, master the art of empathy and accept your true calling!

www.ingramcontent.com/pod-product-compliance
Lightning Source LLC
Chambersburg PA
CBHW060404080526
44583CB00012B/467